W9-BDR-125

Discovering Today's Library

by Alice K. Flanagan and Emily J. Dolbear

Content Advisers:

Ellen Fader, Youth Services Coordinator, Multnomah County Library, Portland, Oregon, and President (2005–06), Association for Library Service to Children, a Division of the American Library Association

Carl A. Harvey II, Library Media Specialist, North Elementary School, Noblesville, Indiana

Gareth Stevens
Publishing

A WEEKLY READER COMPANY

 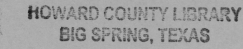

Visit the Gareth Stevens website at: www.garethstevens.com.
For a free color catalog describing Gareth Stevens's list of high-quality
books, call 1-800-542-2595 (USA) or 1-800-387-3178 (Canada).
Gareth Stevens Publishing's fax: (877) 542-2596.

Discovering Today's Library is featured in the Library Skills Kit from
World Almanac Education. Visit the World Almanac Education
website at www.WAEbooks.com. For a free catalog featuring
outstanding books and research skills kits, call 1-800-321-1147.

Library of Congress Cataloging-in-Publication Data
Flanagan, Alice K.
  Discovering today's library / by Alice K. Flanagan and Emily J. Dolbear.
    p. cm.
  Rev. ed. of: Exploring the library. North American ed. 2001.
  Includes bibliographical references and index.
  ISBN-10: 0-8368-7426-9 — ISBN-13: 978-0-8368-7426-6 (lib. bdg.)
  ISBN-10: 0-8368-7427-7 — ISBN-13: 978-0-8368-7427-3 (softcover)
  1. Libraries—Juvenile literature. I. Dolbear, Emily J. II. Flanagan,
Alice K. Exploring the library. III. Title.
  Z665.5.F55   2007
  027—dc22   2006012164

This North American edition first published in 2007 by
Gareth Stevens Publishing
A Weekly Reader® Company
1 Reader's Digest Rd.
Pleasantville, NY 10570-7000 USA

This edition © 2007 by Gareth Stevens Publishing

All photographs © World Almanac Education Group

An Editorial Directions book
Editor: E. Russell Primm, M.A., University of Chicago, Graduate
   Library School
Copy Editors: Irene Keller and Susan Hindman
Indexer: Timothy J. Griffin
Designer: The Design Lab
Photographs by Romie Flanagan, Flanagan Publishing Services

Printed in the United States of America

2 3 4 5 6 7 8 9 10 09 08

We would like to thank the staff of the
following libraries for assisting us in the
production of this book.

Algonquin Public Library

Channing Memorial School

Chicago National College of Naprapathy

Chicago Public Library—Edgebrook Branch

Chicago Public Library—Near North Branch

Dominican University Library

Elmhurst Public Library

Evanston Public Library

Fremont Public Library

John Middleton School

Loyola University School of Law Library

Niles Public Library

Park Ridge Public Library

Table of Contents

INTRODUCTION

Libraries: Windows to the World

Go to a library, and you can take a trip to Mars or scan the ocean floor. With the turn of a page, you can meet the most fascinating people. Some lived in the distant past, and some walk the earth today. In the time it takes to click a mouse, you can travel around the world. Go to a library, and you can read about the best MP3 player or borrow sheet music for a school play.

Fun Fact

U.S. businessman Andrew Carnegie (1835–1919) believed in free libraries. His money built more than 2,500 public libraries around the world!

In a library, you can learn about the present, investigate the past, and plan for the future. Most importantly, you can do all of this in one place.

But a library is more than a building with a wealth of information. It's more than just a place to do your homework or find a fact. A library is an adventure. A library is a window to the world.

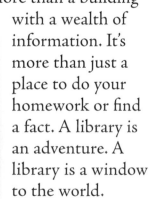

Computers are an important part of modern libraries.

CHAPTER ONE

What Kinds of Libraries Are There?

Libraries are everywhere. Some are on wheels. Some float. Some are behind prison bars. Some are on college campuses. Some are in the offices where people work.

You may even have a library in your own home. Do you have books on a bookshelf? That's a library! Some libraries have no shelves at all. They are completely **electronic**.

The one thing all libraries have in common is that they exist to serve people. These people are called **patrons**. They are also called customers, clients, or users.

Public Libraries

Nearly all people are familiar with public libraries. Most cities and towns in the United States and Canada have public libraries. They are open to everyone, free of charge.

However, it costs lots of money to keep a library open, staffed with people to help and stocked with materials. Most of the money that pays for public libraries comes from the taxes people pay. The rest of the money comes from book sales, donations, contributions from organizations such as Friends of the Library, and **grants** from foundations.

Books are just a part of the many kinds of materials you can explore at the library.

How Many U.S. Public Libraries Are There?

Central or main library buildings. 8,943
Branch libraries 7,147
Total library buildings 16,090

How Many Canadian Public Libraries Are There?

Central and branch library buildings 3,101

Public libraries are designed to serve their communities. For example, a public library in a large city provides materials and programs in many languages. A library in a farming town may have lots of books on agriculture or information on 4-H projects. In Berkeley, California, the public library system runs the Berkeley Tool Library, where patrons can borrow tools!

Libraries in large communities may have many **branches**. Branches are the neighborhood libraries that make up a city or county library system. Smaller towns and cities often have all the library materials and services in one building.

Some public libraries have **bookmobiles**. The first bookmobile was a horse-drawn wagon that carried books in Maryland in 1905! These traveling libraries bring books and other materials to people who may be unable to visit a library building.

These days, a bookmobile might stop near a park to bring picture books, **DVDs**, and games to children or visit a retirement center to bring **large-print books** and sound recordings to seniors. Some bookmobiles offer their patrons Internet access.

Where Are the Five Largest U.S. Public Libraries?

Institution	Volumes
Boston Public Library (Massachusetts)	14,933,349
Chicago Public Library (Illinois)	10,745,608
Public Library of Cincinnati and Hamilton County (Ohio)	9,885,359
Queens Borough Public Library (New York)	9,691,126
County of Los Angeles Public Library (California)	9,185,321

One of the Chicago Public Library's bookmobiles

Fun Fact

The Bill & Melinda Gates Foundation has donated more than 47,000 computers to thousands of public libraries in all fifty states!

Bookmobiles stop at various sites each day for one or two hours. You can call your local library to find out when and where a bookmobile will be in your area.

School Libraries (Library Media Centers)

The library that is most familiar to you is probably your school library. It is also called a **library media center.** A library media center is where many young people first learn about the library and how it works. In fact, you probably visited your school library before you could read!

The United States has more library media centers than any other kind of library. That's because most elementary, middle, junior high, and high schools have a library for their students, teachers, and other staff.

The purpose of school library media centers is to support the **curriculum**—all the subjects you study in your classes. At your library media center, you can find reference materials for

How Many U.S. School Libraries Are There?

Public schools 76,807
Private schools 17,054
Total 93,861

your research report on the shelves and perhaps on the Internet. You might find a **biography** to read for your weekly English paper or a **journal** article that you need to finish your science-fair project. The media center's digital cameras and video equipment are great resources for your **multimedia** class.

Many library media centers also have information about subjects that are not part of the school curriculum. That could include the latest science fiction book by your favorite author, a schedule for local judo classes, or a magazine with a tempting recipe. You can even search an **online database** to find the titles of movies starring an actor you like.

More and more library media centers offer Internet access and computer workstations. With the Internet, you can get a weather forecast for your class field trip or check out news from around the world without getting out of your chair. Your library media center is where you will learn to find and use information of all kinds.

Many school libraries contain computers.

Academic and Research Libraries

Academic libraries are more specialized than your school or local public library. They contain thousands or millions of new and rare books, professional or academic **periodicals**, and online resources. Libraries at colleges and universities serve a community of students and professors as well as some outside researchers and authors. Medical, law, and business schools have libraries, too. These libraries help scholars conduct research that might unearth facts about prehistoric life, result in a faster computer chip, or lead to curing a disease.

Do you know what the library at a historical society does? It preserves information about its state, county, city, or town for researchers and interested community members. If you want to find out how your neighborhood has changed, you might look for historical maps, photographs, and census records at your local historical society's library.

How Many U.S. Academic Libraries Are There?

Less-than-four-year schools 1,379

Four-year and post-graduate schools 2,148

Total 3,527

Where Are the Five Largest U.S. Academic Libraries?

Institution	Volumes
Harvard University	15,181,349
Yale University	11,114,308
University of Illinois—Urbana/Champaign	10,015,321
University of California—Berkeley	9,572,462
University of Texas—Austin	8,322,944

Many cities have private research libraries that are not connected to any larger organization. For example, the Newberry Library in Chicago, Illinois, is an independent research library. Known for its extensive materials on the American West and family history, this private library has more than 1.5 million volumes and 5 million **manuscript** pages.

Special Libraries

Special libraries serve the people in organizations of many sizes. Law firms, automobile companies, advertising agencies, newspapers, religious institutions, book publishers, and zoos usually have special libraries. There are almost ten thousand special libraries in the United States.

Many museums have special libraries, too. Art, science, natural history, and children's museums provide information about a specific subject. While these museum libraries serve their museum workers, other people might use them to learn about new developments in their field, to gather information for

There are thousands of special libraries in the United States.

The Newberry Library is in Chicago.

teaching, or to prepare for special presentations.

Even prisons and ships have libraries. The Folsom State Prison Library in California, for example, lends books and newspapers to its inmates. During visiting hours, prisoners can read to their children. In the library aboard the USS *Abraham Lincoln*, the ship's crew can check out books and keep up with current events.

How Many U.S. Armed Forces and Government Libraries Are There?

Armed forces libraries 314
Government libraries 1,225

Presidential Libraries

Presidential libraries are unique. They collect and maintain materials from a person's presidency. There are twelve of these libraries in the United States. Each presidential library also has a museum that is open to the public.

National Libraries

The Library of Congress is the national library of the United States. It is also the largest library in the world. The federal

Children use a computer to look up information.

government founded this library for members of Congress in 1800. Over time, the library has taken on other important roles. Every day, it receives 22,000 new items and adds about 10,000 of them to its collections. Half of the library's collection is in languages other than English.

Fun Fact

The Library of Congress has about 530 miles (853 kilometers) of bookshelves. That's longer than nine thousand football fields!

The Internet and the Library

The Internet has forever changed people's lives, including the way people use libraries. It allows you to access online information at the library. The Internet also allows you to connect to your public library's **online catalog** and databases from home. If you can't get to your local public library—or if you want to explore a public library thousands of miles away—the Internet will take you there. The Internet can even take you to the Library of Congress at *www.loc.gov*!

The Internet is a network of millions of computers around the world. The part of the Internet that people know best is the World Wide Web. The World Wide Web is the graphical part of the Internet. It is accessed through electronic links that connect directly to other pages of text and images.

There are tens of millions of Web sites. They are run by organizations, companies, schools, or individuals. Many are free, while some provide service for a monthly or yearly fee as a subscription. **Blogs** are one popular kind of Web site. Many individuals create, read, or post replies to these personal online journals.

Since almost anyone can set up a Web site, it is important to check the source of any information you find on the Internet to

Libraries Online Around the World

The Library Index
http://www.libdex.com/
To find your public library's Web page and online catalog

Libweb
http://lists.webjunction.org/libweb/
To find the Web pages and online catalogs of libraries in more than one hundred countries

Lib-Web-Cats
http://www.librarytechnology.org/libwebcats/
To find more than five thousand libraries around the world

National Center for Education Statistics
http://nces.ed.gov/globallocator/
To search for public libraries in the United States

Fun Fact

More than 95 percent of public libraries in the United States offer access to the Internet!

Some Virtual Libraries

ALA Great Web Sites for Kids
http://www.ala.org/greatsites
For homework help and
fun sites

Fact Monster
http://www.factmonster.com/
For an online homework
center and help with writing
and study skills

Internet Public Library
http://www.ipl.org/
For homework help,
references, and a lot
of fun activities

KidsClick!
http://www.kidsclick.org/
For a search site for kids
created by librarians

The Librarians' Internet Index
http://www.lii.org/
For a searchable subject
directory of more than 7,800
Internet resources selected
and evaluated by librarians

The Library Spot
http://www.libraryspot.com/
For dictionaries, encyclopedias, libraries, calculators,
maps, phone books, and
more

be sure it is accurate. Don't trust everything you read online. Ask a **librarian** to help you find reliable sources online as well as in print.

A **virtual library** is a Web site with some of the same reference information—or links to information—as a traditional "bricks-and-mortar" library. Many public, academic, and school libraries set up their own virtual libraries. Whether you are using a virtual or traditional library, you will find the Internet is a valuable tool that can take you almost anywhere.

Home Libraries

Many people have small libraries at home. Many home libraries start out with books that parents buy to read with their children and that children receive as gifts. Later, children need books to help them with their homework. Before long, families have a library of books that inform and entertain. Sometimes favorite books remain with a family for generations.

Some people enjoy building a personal library as a hobby. These people are called **bibliophiles**. They collect books just as others may collect music or movies. Some bibliophiles have so many books that they have to construct a building for their home library!

Do you have a few favorite books at home? Then you have the beginnings of a library. If you expand your collection and keep it in good order, you might create a library that others can use. In 1815, Thomas Jefferson sold his personal collection of books and notes to the young United States. It became the core of the Library of Congress after the British destroyed the original library collection during the War of 1812.

Favorite books can be read over and over again.

Chapter Two

What's in a Library?

Libraries provide a variety of resources to help you learn and have fun. You can read, view, or listen to information at a library. You can find books of all kinds, the latest music **CDs** and movie DVDs, your favorite computer games, and amazing online databases. Most importantly, you can find people to help you in a library!

Books

Books are one of the main resources in a library. People often think of books as falling into two categories: **fiction** and **nonfiction**. All storybooks, folktales, fairy tales, poetry, plays, and novels as well as many picture books are fiction. They are usually invented tales about imaginary characters and events. Nonfiction books provide information about real people and events. Biographies, **autobiographies**, essays, history books, diaries, and some picture books are examples of nonfiction.

Look for the fiction and nonfiction sections in your school or public library. Libraries often have signs pointing out these areas. In many libraries, fiction titles are arranged in alphabetical order according to the author's last name. When it

A librarian helps find a book in a library.

comes to shelving or looking for titles at the library, fiction usually refers only to novels.

Nonfiction books are grouped by subject, according to the **Dewey decimal classification (DDC) system** or the **Library of Congress (LC) classification system**. Each book has a set of numbers and letters, or a **call number**, located on its **spine** to help you find it. (See pages 39–42 for more information.)

(See pages 39–42 for more information.)

> ## Fun Fact
>
> A DVD may look like a CD, but it holds about seven times as much data. Newer DVD formats are being developed to hold even more.

Periodicals

Periodicals are publications published at specified intervals. Newspapers, magazines, and journals are types of periodicals. Newspapers are published most frequently, usually daily or weekly. Magazines are usually published weekly or monthly. Some journals are published only a few times a year.

Some Important U.S. Newspapers

The *Chicago Tribune*
El Diario/La Prensa
The *Los Angeles Times*
The *Miami Herald*
The *New York Times*
The *Washington Post*

Some Popular Magazines for Younger Readers

American Girl
Muse
National Geographic World
Sports Illustrated for Kids
Teen Newsweek
U.S. Kids

Your library might have a list of the hundreds of periodicals to which it subscribes. To help you find information in magazines, you can use an **index** called *The Readers' Guide to Periodical Literature.* Ask a librarian to help you find and use this resource in book form or on the computer.

Libraries subscribe to many newspapers, such as the *New York Times.*

Go to the index and select your topic. The index will list the magazines and newspapers that have published related articles. If the articles are recent, your library might have the printed magazine or newspaper. Some might be available online. Older articles may be kept on filmstrips called **microfilm** or sheets of film called **microfiche.** You have to use special machines to read them.

Some electronic indexes provide more than just references to the information you are looking for. They also include the full texts of some articles. Among the most popular ones are ProQuest, FirstSearch, EBSCO*host,* and HighBeam.

E-books and Audiobooks

Some library collections include electronic books called **e-books.** E-books are books in digital format for display on a computer screen or a handheld device. E-books allow readers to search and retrieve text. An e-book can also be much easier to carry than a large printed reference book.

Some e-books are on **CD-ROM.** Others can be downloaded from the Internet in simple text formats that you can read using a word-processing program. Easy-to-read electronic books are available for palm-sized computers called **PDAs** (personal digital assistants). *Alice in Wonderland* and *The Wizard of Oz* are a few of the many children's books available in this format.

In addition to e-books, libraries provide audiobooks on CD and audiocassette. Some libraries also offer downloadable audiobooks that patrons can listen to on portable digital media players such as iPods as well as on their computers. There are titles for adults, teens, and kids. Some libraries are even lending iPods already loaded with a selection of downloadable books.

Reference Books

To some people, reference books are the most important part of a library. These books represent some of the most-used materials in the library. Although many reference works are available in electronic form, many patrons still rely on the book form. **Encyclopedias, dictionaries** and **thesauruses, atlases** and **gazetteers, almanacs** and **fact books,** and **field guides** are some of the many reference materials you'll find at the library.

Students often use encyclopedias to start their research.

Fun Fact

When was the first general encyclopedia in English issued? The first part of *Encyclopædia Britannica* came out in 1768!

Encyclopedias

Encyclopedias provide information on many topics. The subjects are often arranged in alphabetical order. The two types of encyclopedias are general and special. General encyclopedias include articles on almost any topic you can think of.

Special encyclopedias provide information on specific subjects. They cover topics ranging from computers to comic books, history to horticulture, and medicine to music.

Multivolume encyclopedias are made up of several volumes. Each book has its own number or letter of the alphabet printed on its spine to help users find the information they are seeking. Your school or public library probably has more than one encyclopedia in its collection. Look for them in book form, online, or on DVD.

Dictionaries and Thesauruses

A dictionary lists words in alphabetical order and

Some General Encyclopedias

Columbia Encyclopedia, only online at *http://www. bartleby.com/65/*

Compton's Encyclopedia

Encyclopedia Americana and *The New Book of Knowledge* (also online at *http://go.grolier.com* by subscription)

Encarta, CD/DVD only (also online at *http://www.encarta. msn.com* by subscription; selected information free)

Oxford American Children's Encyclopedia

Scholastic Children's Encyclopedia

World Book (also on CD-ROM and online at *http://www. worldbookonline.com* by subscription)

provides information about each word. You can learn the meaning of the word, its origins, and the year of its first use. A dictionary also tells you how to pronounce the word. Some dictionaries have illustrations.

Many kinds of dictionaries are available today. They include picture dictionaries, children's dictionaries, computer dictionaries, and international-language dictionaries. There are special dictionaries, too. Biographical dictionaries profile famous people in many fields, countries, or time periods. Some dictionaries provide historical facts about the

Some Special Encyclopedias

Baker's Student Encyclopedia of Music

Comic Book Encyclopedia: The Ultimate Guide to Characters, Graphic Novels, Writers, and Artists in the Comic Book Universe

Dinosaur Encyclopedia

Facts on File Encyclopedia of Art

Latin America: History and Culture

The Rolling Stone Encyclopedia of Rock and Roll

Lands and Peoples and *The New Book of Popular Science* (also online at http://go.grolier.com by subscription)

Dictionaries of All Kinds!

DK Children's Illustrated Dictionary

HarperCollins Spanish-English English-Spanish Dictionary

Hippocrene Children's Illustrated Chinese (Mandarin) Dictionary

Hippocrene Children's Illustrated Russian Dictionary

Merriam-Webster's Collegiate Dictionary (also on CD-ROM and online at http://www.merriam-webstercollegiate.com by subscription)

Oxford English Dictionary (also on CD-ROM)

Random House Japanese-English English-Japanese Dictionary

Scholastic Dictionary of Spelling

Webster's New World Student Dictionary

United States or other countries of the world. Many libraries even have sign language dictionaries.

Thesauruses are usually shelved near the dictionaries. A thesaurus is a listing of words with their synonyms (words with the same or nearly the same meaning).

Atlases and Gazetteers

An atlas is a book of maps. An atlas may feature road maps, maps that show specific countries and states, weather maps, population maps, illustrated maps, or historical maps. The *Atlas of the North American Indian* shows you where major North American Indian tribes lived throughout history and gives some information about their contemporary lives. You can find all kinds of atlases in a library, including atlases for small towns, the world, and even space. There is even an atlas about law breaking called *The Historical Atlas of American Crime*!

A gazetteer provides population figures and other basic facts about cities, towns, and regions of the world. It can also provide information about flags. This is a terrific source for current facts when you are doing a report on a state or country.

Some Atlases

Atlas of American History

Children's Night Sky Atlas

DK World Atlas (on CD-ROM as *3D World Atlas*)

Rand McNally Kids' Road Atlas

World Almanac Children's Atlas of the United States

Some Online Gazetteers

U.S. Gazetteer

http://www.census.gov/cgi-bin/gazetteer/index.html

For U.S. Census Bureau data by city or town

World Gazetteer

http://www.world-gazetteer.com

For population data and related statistics by country

Almanacs and Fact Books

Almanacs provide facts at a glance. They answer questions such as: What are the three largest cities in the United States? What is the tallest building in the world? (In case you're wondering, according to the latest U.S. Census Bureau population estimates found on *www.worldalmanacforkids.com*, New York City, Los Angeles, and Chicago are the three largest U.S. cities. The site also lists Taiwan's Taipei 101 as the tallest building in the world today.)

Almanacs and Fact Books

ESPN Information Please Sports Almanac

The Old Farmer's Almanac for Kids (also online at *http://www.almanac4kids.com*)

The World Almanac and Book of Facts

The World Almanac for Kids (also online at *http://www.worldalmanacforkids.com*)

The World Factbook (also online at *http://www.odci.gov/cia/publications/factbook*)

Almanacs, full of general facts and statistics, are usually updated every year.

Field guides offer lots of useful information about the world of nature.

Many different kinds of almanacs and fact books are available today. *The World Factbook*, published by the Central Intelligence Agency, has useful information about the nations of the world. Most fact books are updated each year. Ask your librarian to show you an almanac or a fact book just for kids.

Out in the Field

National Audubon Society Field Guide to North American Butterflies

Peterson First Guide to Reptiles and Amphibians

The Sibley Guide to Birds

Simon & Schuster's Children's Guide to Insects and Spiders

Field Guides

Field guides are reference books about nature. They help you learn about the plants and animals in a park or your backyard. Field guides are filled with **range maps**, pictures, charts, illustrations, and useful terms. These books tell you all about birds, animal tracks, insects, flowers, rocks and minerals, and even snakes.

Other Reference Books

Your library has lots of other reference materials, of course. Many of them are written especially for or appeal to young people. You can read the life stories of thousands of authors and artists in the online and print series called *Something about the Author.* You can research the past with *Climbing Your Family Tree: Online and Off-line Genealogy for Kids.* To improve your classroom and creative composition, you can look for *Writer's Express: A Handbook for Young Writers, Thinkers, and Learners.*

Check out *Kids in Print: Publishing a School Newspaper* if you have ever thought of starting up a publication at your school. Or

The library has reference books on topics of all kinds.

read through *A Kid's Guide to Creating Web Pages for Home and School* for details about starting a school Web site. Whatever your interests are, you can locate information at the library to help expand your knowledge.

Online Resources

Many wonderful online resources are available at your library. Many libraries have their own Web pages. These pages can be great starting points for information searches. A library's Web page allows you access to its online databases, large collections of information organized for quick search and retrieval. You can search databases of magazine and newspaper articles, encyclopedia entries, and entire works of literature. Home access to these databases is often available for library members with a valid library card number.

At the library or home, you can also use **search engines** or **directories** to look for information on the Internet. A search engine looks for **keywords** on Web sites all over the World Wide Web. A directory is a listing of Web sites that can be searched for specific topics. The Internet has dozens of search engines and directories, some general and others specialized to index specific subjects. They can help you search millions and millions of Web sites. Google is the largest Internet search engine with more than 2 billion indexed pages!

Some Biographical Series

Biography Today

Book of Junior Authors and Illustrators

Contemporary Black Biography
    (also online at *http://www.gale.com/gvrl/* by subscription)

Current Biography
    (also online at *http://www.hwwilson.com/* by subscription)

Favorite Children's Authors and Illustrators

Something about the Author
    (also online at *http://www.gale.com/gvrl/* by subscription)

Search engines on the Internet make finding information easy.

You type in a keyword or a phrase to begin your search. The search engine or directory will pull up a list of Web sites that should be related to your topic of research. You may have to narrow or broaden your search by using a shorter phrase or more general keyword. Unlike a library's Web page, some Web sites provide incorrect information. Don't forget to check with your librarian about the best online sources for you to use.

Fun Fact

The last three letters of a Web address give clues about the site's organizer: *edu* (educational institution), *com* (commercial organization), *gov* (government or agency in the United States), and *mil* (U.S. military).

When you are online, you can get help with homework, too. Some libraries offer a service that matches students with real tutors online. You can also find information in many forms, including words, pictures, sound, and video. You can search books, newspapers, magazines, pictures, maps, or TV and radio. You can even print out the answers to your research questions.

Some Internet Search Engines and Directories

Ask for Kids
http://www.askforkids.com

Awesome Library
http://www.awesomelibrary.org/

Dogpile
http://www.dogpile.com

Google
http://www.google.com

MSN Search
http://search.msn.com

Yahoo!
http://search.yahoo.com

Yahooligans!
http://www.yahooligans.com

Chapter Three

Mapping Out the Library

A library has several special areas. Each section has its own purpose. Sometimes each section has specially trained professionals and **clerks**. The areas you will probably use most often are the lending areas, the periodicals area, and the reference area.

The lending areas have all the items that can be borrowed for a specified amount of time (usually from one to three weeks). That includes hardcover and paperback books, videos, audiocassettes, and DVDs. You will find a **library catalog** of all the library's materials in this area. (If your library has an online catalog, you usually can also access it from computers in different parts of the building.) The lending areas can include the adult, children's and teens', and **audiovisual** and multimedia sections.

Adult Section

The adult section has books for older readers. It is usually divided into fiction, or novels, and nonfiction. Many libraries have a separate area for biographies. Fiction is often shelved alphabetically by the author's last name. Nonfiction, poetry, and plays are shelved using the DDC system or LC classification system (see pages 39–42 for more information).

Using the library catalog helps to find items in the library's collection.

Children's and Teens' Sections

Almost every public library has a children's section for its younger patrons. In this part of the library, you may find a few **board books** or games for your afternoon babysitting job, a manga magazine for yourself, or a new DVD to watch over the weekend.

Librarians try to make this area as inviting as possible. Materials are kept on shelves that kids can easily reach. Books are sometimes shelved according to reading difficulty or type. Many children's areas have special racks for the most popular books and subjects.

The fiction section, which has mostly novels, is often shelved in alphabetical order by the author's last name. Nonfiction (or information) books are usually grouped by subject. Each book has a call number on its spine to tell you where it belongs. The letters J or JUV (Juvenile), YP (Young Person), YA (Young Adult), or E (Everybody) let you know that the book is intended for young people.

Some public libraries have young adult sections for teens. Here young people might find comic books and graphic novels, science fiction and fantasy books, young adult novels, and their own magazine section. Young adult sections often have their own computer workstations for Internet research and browsing.

Libraries usually have entire sections for children's books.

VENILE
N-FICTION

A - E

Young Adult
Fiction
and
Teen Edition

Young adult books are sometimes
shelved in their own area.

Audiovisual and Multimedia Section

The audiovisual and multimedia section of a library is a popular
area. Some libraries provide listening and viewing stations. Here
you can listen to music cassettes and CDs, books on tape, and
international-language tapes. You might also be able to play
educational computer games or try out new software programs.
Some libraries allow patrons to check out movies on videotape or
DVD to watch at home.

Periodicals Area

In this part of the library, you might find patrons in comfortable
chairs reading *YM* magazine or a local newspaper. The area has
magazines, newspapers, and journals on many subjects for a
variety of readers. The periodicals area is intended to provide both
entertainment and information.

Computers in the library can also be used for music and games!

Display racks hold the current issue of each periodical with a few **back issues** stacked behind it or on a rack below. Some libraries lend the back issues. You might have to go to the reference area to look at periodicals from past years on microfilm or microfiche. Most libraries also have online periodical databases.

Reference Area

The reference area is a center of activity. The phone is constantly ringing with calls from patrons with questions. Other patrons are using online catalogs, reading at desks, and requesting materials from other libraries through **interlibrary loan**. A high school student might be learning about his family history using microfilm of census records. A young woman might be researching how to start her own business at a computer workstation. A retired person might be reading *Value Line's Investment Survey* and annual reports from corporations, or a young boy might be researching the value of his baseball card and Hot Wheels collections. All of these activities make the reference area a very busy place.

The heart of the reference area, however, is the reference desk. The **reference librarians** are trained to help people find the answers they need. These librarians surround themselves with ready reference materials—the books and online sources that help them answer the most commonly asked questions. Some public libraries are even equipping reference librarians and **library assistants** with headsets so that they don't have to stay at the reference desk. These roving staff members help people wherever they are in the library.

Materials in the reference area are called **noncirculating items.** They are kept in the library all the time so that patrons and librarians always have access to them. They include encyclopedias, almanacs, atlases, and dictionaries of all kinds. Many libraries put "R" or "REF" on the spines of reference books to tell you that they cannot be taken out of the library.

Many public libraries offer Internet access terminals. They may be located in the reference section of the library, in their own special area, or throughout the library. Ask the library staff where they are in your library.

Librarians are ready to help patrons find what they need.

Viewing a special exhibit at the library

Other Areas

Many public libraries have exhibits that change regularly. They display items from their own collections or another library's collection or even items from community members. Exhibits might include local historical photographs or artifacts. A special exhibit in the children's section might have an antique doll collection or a tank full of exotic fish.

Libraries may also offer quiet reading rooms, meeting rooms for local organizations, study centers for young adults, or a storytelling room for children. Some libraries even have small auditoriums for film screenings, guest speakers, and live performances. Have you been to the library lately? It may not be the place you think it is!

Behind the Scenes

Behind the scenes, library workers keep the library running. Librarians do many things that you might not know about. For example, librarians order, **catalog**, and manage their collection of materials. They are also responsible for managing a portion of the library's budget.

In a part of the library closed to the public, staff members decide which books to repair or rebind. They also decide which materials to remove permanently from the library. This process is

Braille books let
visually impaired
people read by touch.

called **weeding**. Librarians remove materials that are no longer up-to-date. They also weed out materials damaged beyond repair and materials too fragile for the public to use. Librarians need to make space for the new books, CDs, and DVDs that you want to borrow.

Special Services

Some library patrons have disabilities. For those who are homebound, some libraries offer home service. Many patrons who are visually or hearing impaired use special services at the library.

At many public libraries, patrons with visual impairments use large-print books, magnifiers, and computers with large screens. They listen through headphones to reading machines or computers that convert printed words into speech. Some visually impaired people read **braille** books by moving their fingertips lightly across lines of raised dots. Each number and letter of the alphabet has its own pattern of dots.

Patrons with hearing impairments use headphones that amplify speech on computers and books on CDs. Some libraries also have videos with captions that describe the action. With advance notice, some libraries will provide an American Sign Language (ASL) interpreter. Ask at your library to learn about the special services it offers.

Fun Fact

What country has the highest percentage of registered library borrowers? Finland, with about 45 percent!

Circulation Desk

The first and last place you see in the library is probably the circulation desk. This is where you present your library card and borrow the **circulating items** that you have chosen. You may have a pile of picture books for your sister or brother, nonfiction materials to help you with a school project, or a movie to watch with your friends.

Libraries check out items in different ways. Some libraries still use the pocket method. In this method, every circulating item has a paper pocket. In a library book, the pocket is usually on the first or last page. A clerk stamps the due date on a card and puts it in the pocket. This library worker also scans the item's **bar code** into the computer and your library card number to keep a record of the books you borrow. In addition, the clerk can tell you if you have any books that have not been returned.

Many public libraries no longer use the pocket method. Instead, they just scan the bar code and stamp a return date on the inside cover of the book. Some use another method. After they scan a bar code, they give a paper receipt to the borrower that shows when the book must be returned. Other libraries have **self-checkout machines**!

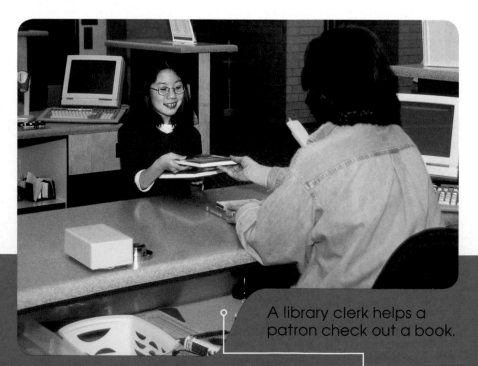

A library clerk helps a patron check out a book.

Chapter Four

Everything in Its Place (and How to Find It)

Libraries often have thousands or even millions of items. How do librarians organize, store, and retrieve all those items? And how can you find what you are looking for at the library? Librarians could arrange the items by the physical size of the item or by publisher or by publication date. Over the years, however, librarians have developed classifications based on subject for the nonfiction materials. Fiction is usually arranged alphabetically by the author's last name.

Libraries in the United States, Canada, and other English-speaking countries often use either the Dewey decimal classification (DDC) system or the Library of Congress (LC)

A librarian can use a computer catalog to check up on library materials.

classification system. In both systems, the library keeps a catalog that lists every item in its collection, and each item has a **call number**. The call number helps you find the item on the shelves.

The Library Catalog

Librarians use an online catalog to find items, monitor the collection, and check the dates when materials are due back. Patrons use the catalog to locate items of interest on the shelves. In the past, the catalog was kept on index cards in file drawers. A few libraries still use this **card catalog** method, but most school and public libraries now use online catalogs.

You can search a library catalog in a number of ways. Author, title, subject, and keyword are the most common, but you can also search by series title, illustrator, or coauthor.

nonfiction
001. - 398.2 H

nonfiction
398.2 I - 599.8

Signs help this young patron find the book she's looking for.

You will see the call number on the computer screen or in the upper left of the catalog card. After you find your call number (and write it down!), follow signs to the row of shelves that contains your call number. Then you can **browse** through the shelves to find what you are looking for. Always ask for help if you can't find what you want. Check with the reference librarian if what you need isn't in your library. It may be available from another library through interlibrary loan.

The Dewey Decimal Classification System

Most school and public libraries organize their books by the Dewey decimal classification system. Melvil Dewey invented this system in 1876. Under this system, books are divided into ten main groups or classes. Each class is identified by a set of numbers. Each class is then divided into ten subclasses. (See pages 40–41 for the complete list.) The original classification system was published in a forty-two page booklet. In today's information-rich world, the Dewey decimal classification system fills four volumes and almost four thousand pages!

(text continues on p. 42)

Some Dewey Call Numbers

The World Almanac for Kids	j 031 Wor*
Favorite Greek Myths by Mary Pope Osborne	j 292 Osb
Say Hola to Spanish by Susan Middleton Elya	j 463 Ely
Destination: Jupiter by Seymour Simon	j 523.45 Sim
Gorillas by Paul Fleisher	j 599.884 Fle
I Is for Idea: An Inventions Alphabet by Marcia Schonberg	j 600 Sch
Unlikely Pairs: Fun with Famous Works of Art by Bob Raczka	j 750.22 Rac
Where the Sidewalk Ends by Shel Silverstein	j 811 Sil

*j means juvenile

000 General Knowledge (Almanacs, Encyclopedias, Libraries, Museums, Newspapers, etc.)
010 Bibliographies
020 Library & Information Science
030 General Encyclopedias
040 (Not used)
050 General Periodicals
060 General Organizations & Museums
070 Journalism & Publishing
080 Collections
090 Manuscripts and Rare Books

100 Psychology and Philosophy (Death & Dying, Ethics, Feelings, Logic, Making Friends, Optical Illusions, Superstitions)
110 Metaphysics
120 Epistemology
130 Paranormal Phenomena & Occult
140 Specific Philosophies
150 Psychology
160 Logic
170 Ethics
180 Ancient, Medieval & Oriental Philosophy
190 Modern Western Philosophy

200 Religions and Mythology (Amish, Bible Stories, Christianity, Judaism, Islam, Quakers, Shakers)
210 Natural Religion
220 Bible
230 Christian Theology
240 Christian Moral Theology
250 Local Church & Religious Orders
260 Social & Ecclesiastical Theology
270 History & Geography of Church
280 Christian Denominations & Sects
290 Non-Christian & Comparative Religion

300 Social Sciences and Folklore (Careers, Customs, Environment, Families, Government, Manners, Money, Recycling)
310 Statistics
320 Political Science
330 Economics
340 Law
350 Public Administration
360 Social Concerns & Services
370 Education

380 Trade & Commerce
390 Customs, Etiquette, Folklore

400 Languages and Grammar (Chinese, English, French, German, Italian, Japanese, Sign Language, Spanish)
410 Linguistics
420 English Language
430 Germanic & Scandinavian Languages
440 French
450 Italian
460 Spanish & Portuguese
470 Latin
480 Classical Greek
490 Other Languages

500 Math and Science (Animals, Biology, Chemistry, Dinosaurs, Fish, Geology, Insects, Physics, Planets, Plants)
510 Math
520 Astronomy
530 Physics
540 Chemistry
550 Earth Science
560 Paleontology
570 Life Sciences
580 Botany
590 Zoology

600 Medicine and Technology (Computers, Engineering, Farming, Health, Human Body, Manufacturing, Nutrition)

610 Medicine
620 Engineering
630 Agriculturo
640 Home Economics
650 Management
660 Chemical Technologies
670 Manufacturing
680 Application-Specific Manufacturing
690 Building

700 Arts & Recreation (Architecture, Crafts, Drawing, Games, Jokes, Music, Puppets, Songbooks, Sports)

710 Civic & Landscape Art
720 Architecture
730 Sculpture
740 Drawing
750 Painting
760 Graphic & Printed Art
770 Photography
780 Music
790 Sports & Recreation

800 Literature (Children's Literature, Plays, Poetry, Shakespeare, Writing)

810 American Literature
820 English Literature
830 Germanic Literature
840 French Literature
850 Italian Literature
860 Spanish & Portuguese Literature
870 Latin Literature
880 Classical Greek Literature
890 Literature of Other Languages

900 Geography and History (Biographies, Countries, Native Americans, States, Travel, Wars)

910 Travel & Geography
920 Genealogy & Geography
930 Ancient History
940 European History
950 Asian History
960 African History
970 North American History
980 South American History
990 History of Other Areas

Each of the subclassifications is further subdivided. Sports & Recreation, for example, is subdivided as follows:

790 Sports & Recreation
791 Public Performances
792 Stage Presentations
793 Indoor Games & Amusements
794 Indoor Games of Skill
795 Games of Chance
796 Athletic & Outdoor Sports & Games
797 Aquatic & Air Sports
798 Equestrian Sports & Animal Racing
799 Fishing, Hunting & Shooting

With the use of a decimal point and extra digits after the point, each of these sections can be further subdivided to cover increasingly narrower subject areas. For example, for Athletic & Outdoor Sports & Games:

796.3 Ball Games
796.32 Inflated Ball Hit or Thrown by Hand
796.323 Basketball
796.3232 Strategy & Tactics

The Dewey decimal system includes a wide variety of subjects.

The Library of Congress Classification System

Some large public libraries and many research libraries use the Library of Congress classification system. This system divides knowledge into twenty-one main classes. A single letter identifies each class. If you have trouble finding a call number, ask a librarian to help you.

Subject Headings in Library Catalogs

Many items in the library contain information about a number of different subjects. To help patrons find all the works that might relate to what they are looking for, librarians assign several subject

Some Library of Congress Subject Headings

Parks, Rosa, 1913–2005—Juvenile literature

Piglets—Juvenile literature

Presidents—United States—Biography—Juvenile literature

Winter—Juvenile literature

headings to each item in the library catalog. These headings may be a single word, many words, or even phrases that help describe the work's content. With online catalogs, patrons can search for materials using these subject terms.

Some Sears List Subject Headings

Hispanic Americans—Biography

Kennedy, John F. (John Fitzgerald), 1917–1963

Science fiction—History and criticism

In the United States, libraries use two main systems for creating subject headings: the Library of Congress and the Sears List of Subject Headings. The Library of Congress headings are used mainly by academic libraries, public libraries, and special libraries. School library media centers often use the Sears List heading.

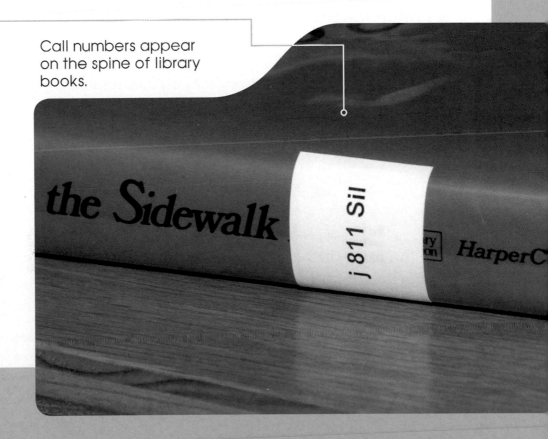

Call numbers appear on the spine of library books.

Chapter Five

Who Can Help You at the Library?

If you need help at the library, many people can assist you. The most important part of a librarian's job is helping the public use the library. Librarians also order materials, catalog books, and work at the reference desk. They organize exhibits and special library events, including **book clubs**, storytelling, and special performances for children. Before the end of the day, librarians in large libraries may have helped hundreds of people in person, on the phone, and online.

At the Public Library

A large public library may have several librarians, assistants, and clerks to help you. They work as a team. Each person has a different job to do. Sometimes librarians take turns doing certain jobs. However, some small public libraries have only one librarian to run the whole library.

How Many People Work in U.S. Libraries?

	Librarians	Other Paid Staff	Total Staff
Academic Libraries	25,152	70,291	95,443
Public Libraries	45,115	91,057	136,172
School Libraries	66,471	99,557	166,028
Total	136,738	260,905	397,643*

*Figures for special libraries are not available, although the Special Library Association has 15,000 professional members who work in special libraries. The total number of people employed in special libraries is certainly higher.

Librarians work to help patrons use the library.

The following are a few of the many jobs librarians, assistants, and clerks perform. Librarians select new materials. Before you can borrow the materials, they give each item a call number and add it to the library catalog. These librarians are called **catalogers**.

Librarians who specialize in finding information are called reference librarians. Most usually have master's degrees in **library science**. Some have other graduate degrees, too. Reference librarians answer questions about almost anything. They help people use the catalog and find library materials and online information.

Librarians in the children's section of a library may have a helper who is familiar with children's books and other materials. A children's or youth librarian can recommend a good book to read for fun or to use as research for school projects. Librarians show you how to use the computers.

Library assistants or clerks at the circulation desk of a library can be most helpful. If a library has no self-checkout machines, these workers can check out hundreds of items a day. Each transaction is recorded in the computer—usually when the item is checked out and returned. They provide help with your library account. During the busiest times of the day, several people may be working at the circulation desk.

The workers who put books and magazines back on the library shelves are called **shelvers** or **pages**. They carefully return items to their proper places in the library after patrons are finished reading them so that other people using the library can find them.

Some libraries hire specialists to help their patrons. A specialist might take care of the library's audiovisual equipment. Other specialists might help patrons find information on the Internet. But all librarians have to be informed about the latest technology and software programs.

A library assistant applies a shelving label to the spine of a new book.

At the School Library (or Library Media Center)

At the school library or library media center, librarians are often called **library media specialists** or teacher-librarians. Library media specialists are responsible for helping students learn how to find and use information. They work with classroom teachers to help students practice those skills. They also make sure the media center has plenty of materials on topics covered in the classroom. Sometimes volunteers, assistants, or part-time clerks help the library media specialists. In very small schools, the person operating the library might be a volunteer.

Most library media centers are not open to the general public. While a public library serves all people in a community, a library media center exists for only the school's teachers, students and

One task for school library helpers is reshelving materials.

Library media specialists help students use the school library.

their parents, and staff. With such a focused group of users, a library media center and its staff can concentrate on the needs of the students and teachers. If you are looking for resources that aren't available at the school library, a library media specialist will often direct you to a local public or research library.

Library media specialists have special training in their field. They often hold degrees in education or library science. Sometimes a library media specialist has master's degrees in both education and library science.

Library media specialists have an enormous job. They plan and run most aspects of their school's library program. A typical day might include reading an Eric Carle story to kindergarteners, working in the computer lab with a fourth-grade class, and teaching fifth-graders how to use an encyclopedia for their reports on a U.S. president.

Library media specialists help you learn the skills you need to become effective users of information. These skills can help you use the library to do your schoolwork more efficiently. With these skills, you can also discover new novelists, learn more about your pen pal's country, or locate results for snowboarding events at the most recent Winter X Games.

Between group activities, library media specialists are selecting and cataloging new materials. They or their helpers are checking out books, recording returns, and keeping the library in order. They are also there to help you find books—fiction and nonfiction—that you'll enjoy for pleasure reading. After school, many library media specialists put in extra time in the library making displays or advising teachers on classroom projects.

Now and then, library media specialists organize a special library event, such as a family reading night or a schoolwide book swap. They also organize the school's summer reading program. Although library media specialists are busy, they are there to help you learn more about the library and the world around you.

A library media specialist teaches students in a computer lab.

Chapter Six

What's Going On at the Library?

There's more going on at the library than research and reading. Libraries are exciting places in many ways. Public libraries are the heart of the community, where the arts, education, and entertainment thrive.

The next time you're in a public library, ask the librarian about upcoming events. Or pick up an activity calendar. Check to see if your library has its calendar online. Find out what's going on at your library!

Often local artists and photographers display their work at the library. Actors, musicians, and storytellers sometimes visit libraries to put on performances or puppet shows. Librarians invite authors and illustrators to talk about their books and

An author talks to children about his book.

Some libraries run chess clubs for interested players.

read from them. They might even sell copies of their books and autograph them. Libraries with auditoriums sometimes put on film programs.

Throughout the year, many libraries offer literacy education, study classes, chess clubs, or craft programs. Many provide homework help for children and computer research online. Some libraries sponsor book clubs for children, teens, and adults. The book club members meet at the library to discuss the books they have read.

Most public libraries organize summer reading programs for children. Some offer infant programs for babies and their parents. These programs help parents learn nursery rhymes and songs to share with their babies and introduce infants to the library. One of the library's most popular events is story time, when the librarian reads stories to children.

Often, libraries have used book sales. School libraries have book fairs at which parents, teachers, and children buy books. Libraries also hold job fairs to help people learn about new careers. Often community groups hold meetings in the library. There's always something happening at a library!

The next time you go to your public or school library, make it an adventure. Explore all the different areas. Observe what people are doing and how they are learning. Ask questions. Make at least one interesting discovery, and learn how to do one new thing. Discovering everything that today's library offers can be fun.

Librarians help students in many ways.

Chapter Seven

Tips on How to Behave at the Library and Online

Libraries are places of learning. Here are some tips on the proper way to behave in a library.

- If you have to wait for a librarian to help you, be patient. Remember to thank a librarian for his or her help.
- Be polite. Wait your turn for materials.
- Share materials. Don't keep materials longer than necessary. You are not the only person who needs them.
- Help others. This makes using the library an enjoyable experience.

A librarian shows a young patron how to use an online catalog.

- Treat the books and other materials gently and with respect. Remember, the library belongs to everyone.
- Keep your workplace clean. Pick up after yourself before you leave. Others have to use the space after you.
- Follow library rules and obey library workers. They are in charge of the library.
- Return all items to their proper place. Some libraries do not want you to return books and materials to the shelves. Look for signs that tell you where to leave the books that you don't want to check out.

You might use the Internet at your school library or local public library—or at home. Here are some tips on the proper way to behave online:

- Follow the library rules for using the Internet. Follow your family's Internet rules at home. If you don't have any home rules, create a list with your parents. You could probably teach them a lot about how the Internet works!
- Talk to a librarian or your parents about what you are doing on the Internet. Ask for help finding information. Tell a trusted adult about anything you find on the Internet that makes you uncomfortable.
- Be polite on the Internet. Treat others online as if you were talking to them in person.

Using the Internet
at a library
computer

* Never give your personal information to strangers on the Internet. That includes your name, address, phone number, school's name and address, passwords, or personal photographs.
* Respond only to e-mails from friends and family. Don't ever make plans to meet a person you know only from the Internet. Tell your parents immediately if anyone you met online wants to get together.

- Don't ever open e-mail attachments from people you don't know. They might contain computer viruses that could damage a computer.
- Don't hog the computer at home or at the library. Your family members, classmates, or other library patrons want to do research, send e-mails, or chat online, too.
- Remember that not everything you find on the Internet is reliable or accurate. Most blogs and home pages as well as many Web sites are run by individuals. The information can be false, out-of-date, or biased.
- Have fun on the Internet. Use it to do interesting research for your school projects, read blogs about your favorite hobbies, and e-mail pictures of your new pets to your grandparents. The Internet is an incredible resource. Make the most of it!

A library is a window to the world.

Glossary

almanacs—books of general facts and statistics published once a year

atlases—books of maps

audiovisual—related to both hearing and sight

autobiographies—books in which the writer tells the story of his or her own life

back issues—previous editions of a magazine or journal

bar code—a band of lines containing information that can be read by a computer

bibliophiles—people who love collecting and reading books

biography—a book that tells someone's life story

blogs—personal online journals

board books—picture books made of heavy cardboard

book clubs—groups whose members read books and discuss them in person or online

bookmobiles—buses or vans used as traveling libraries

braille—a system of writing used by people who have visual impairments; it uses raised dots that are felt by the fingertips

branches—the neighborhood libraries that are part of a city's or county's library system

browse—to look over casually in search of something of interest

call number—a combination of numbers and letters that indicate where a book should be shelved in a library

card catalog—index cards that list all a library's materials

catalog—to give each item a call number and place it in the library's list of holdings

catalogers—library workers who give each item a call number and list it in the library catalog

CDs (compact discs)—small plastic discs that store information and music digitally

CD-ROM (compact discs read-only memory)—a compact disc that produces words and pictures and is used on a computer

circulating items—items that can be borrowed from a library

clerks—library workers who check books in and out, empty the book drop, help order materials, and do other tasks to help librarians

curriculum—a course of study

Dewey decimal classification (DDC) system—a method of organizing library materials that divides knowledge into ten main classes

dictionaries—listings of words in alphabetical order along with their forms, pronunciations, and meanings

directories—Web sites of categories and lists of other Web sites

DVDs (digital versatile discs)—small plastic discs that store more digital information than CD-ROMs

e-books—books in digital format for display on a computer screen or a handheld device

electronic—powered by electricity

encyclopedias—books or sets of books containing information on many subjects and usually organized alphabetically

fact books—listings of information on general subjects

fiction—writings about characters and events from the imagination

field guides—handbooks used to identify plant and animal life in nature

gazetteers—geographical dictionaries

grants—gifts of money from the government or other organizations for a particular purpose

index—an alphabetical listing of the information in a book or other reference

interlibrary loan—the process of borrowing materials from other libraries

journal—a professional or academic periodical

keywords—words entered into a search engine or an online catalog to retrieve information on a particular subject

large-print books—books with print large enough for people with visual impairments to read

librarian—a person who specializes in the care or management of a library

library assistants—people who work alongside reference librarians at the reference desk to help out with many routine requests

library catalog—a listing (on printed cards or online) of all a library's materials

library media center—a school library

library media specialists—school librarians

Library of Congress (LC) classification system—a method of organizing library materials that divides knowledge into twenty-one main classes

library science—the study of library work

manuscript—an original written composition of something before it is published

microfiche—a sheet of film of pictures of printed pages

microfilm—a filmstrip of pictures of printed pages

multimedia—using various kinds of technologies such as video, sound, and text

noncirculating items—materials in the reference section of a library that cannot be borrowed

nonfiction—writing that tells about real people, things, and events, such as biographies, autobiographies, essays, history books, diaries, and some picture books

online catalog—a computer listing of all the materials a library owns

online database—a site with a large collection of information organized for quick search and retrieval

pages—library workers who shelve materials in the proper place; also called shelvers

patrons—people who use a library

PDAs (personal digital assistants)—palm-sized computers used for storing and organizing personal information; newer PDAs can be used as mobile phones, web browsers, or media players

periodicals—publications published at specified intervals

range maps—colored drawings that show where animals live or trees grow

reference librarians—librarians who specialize in finding information

search engines—software programs that search the Internet for Web sites containing keywords

self-checkout machines—machines that allow library patrons to check out library materials without the help of a library worker

shelvers—library workers who shelve materials in the proper place; also called pages

special libraries—libraries that serve members of organizations of many sizes

spine—the part of a book cover where the pages attach and the book title usually appears

thesauruses—books that list words with their synonyms

virtual library—a Web site with some of the same reference information—or links to information—as a traditional "bricks-and-mortar" library

weeding—removing permanently or discarding items from a library collection

A Short History of Libraries

More than 30,000 years ago	Early man paints pictures on the walls of caves to explain events. It could be said that these caves were the first libraries.
5000 BC	Egyptians record their history on a type of paper called papyrus. The papyrus sheets are rolled into long scrolls and kept in the Pharoahs' palaces, temples, and tombs.
About 3000 BC	The people of Mesopotamia (now Iraq) begin etching pictures on clay tablets to record events, laws, and business transactions.
300s BC	The Greeks make libraries available to everyone. One of the most famous Greek libraries is in Alexandria, Egypt. It may have had more than 500,000 papyrus scrolls.
221–206 BC	The first libraries in China begin. The finest library belongs to the Emperor of China. It was called the Imperial Library.
200 BC to AD 476	The Romans build many beautiful libraries.
1366	The first European national library is founded in Prague, in what is now the Czech Republic.
About 1450	The German inventor Johannes Gutenberg perfects a way to print books using a press and small pieces of metal type. His invention makes it easy to create multiple copies of a book.
Late 1500s–Early 1600s	Europeans settle in North America and bring a few religious books with them, which they share with friends.
About 1638	A printing press is shipped from England to Cambridge, Massachusetts. Harvard College opens a library with three hundred books. It is the first true library in the United States.
1731	Benjamin Franklin founds the Library Company of Philadelphia. It is the first society library in the United States. (A society library was made up of personal libraries and sold shares. Money raised from the shares was then used to buy more books.)
1800	The U.S. government founds a library for members of Congress, called the Library of Congress.

1812	The British destroy the Library of Congress collection in the War of 1812. (In 1815, Thomas Jefferson sells his books and notes to the U.S. government, which become the core of a new Library of Congress.)
1833	The oldest tax-supported public library in the United States begins in Peterborough, New Hampshire. The Peterborough Public Library is still open today.
1836	The U.S. government establishes the National Library of Medicine.
1848	The Boston Public Library is established and quickly becomes the model for other public libraries in the United States by allowing patrons to take books home.
1876	Melvil Dewey invents the Dewey decimal classification (DDC) system.
1886	The Library of Congress moves into its new home, the Thomas Jefferson Building.
Early 1900s	The Library of Congress begins developing its own classification system.
1938	The Library of Congress opens its second building—the John Adams Building.
1980	The third, and largest, of the Library of Congress's buildings opens—the James Madison Building.
1994	The U.S. government establishes the National Library of Education.
2004	The William J. Clinton Presidential Library and Museum opens in Little Rock, Arkansas. It is the largest presidential library in the United States.
2005	Public libraries in fourteen Louisiana parishes are seriously damaged or destroyed during hurricanes Katrina and Rita. Many of their collections are lost.
TODAY	The Library of Congress in Washington, D.C., is the world's largest library. It holds more than 130 million items.

For More Information about the Library

Books

Appelt, Kathi. *Down Cut Shin Creek: The Pack Horse Librarians of Kentucky.* New York: HarperCollins Children's Books, 2001.

Heiligman, Deborah. *The New York Public Library's Guide to Research.* New York: Scholastic Reference, 1998.

Pearson, Debora, ed., *When I Went to the Library: Writers Celebrate Books and Reading.* Berkeley, Calif.: Groundwood Books, 2002.

Raatma, Lucia. *Safety on the Internet.* Chanhassen, Minn.: Child's World, 2005.

Rau, Dana Meachen. *Andrew Carnegie: Captain of Industry.* Minneapolis: Compass Point Books, 2006.

Ruurs, Margriet. *My Librarian Is a Camel: How Books Are Brought to Children Around the World.* Honesdale, Pa.: Boyds Mills Press, 2005.

Santella, Andrew. *The Library of Congress.* Minneapolis: Compass Point Books, 2006.

Sherman, Josepha. *Internet Safety.* Danbury, Conn.: Franklin Watts, 2003.

Simon, Charnan. *Andrew Carnegie: Builder of Libraries.* Danbury, Conn.: Children's Press, 1998.

Stamaty, Mark Alan. *Alia's Mission: Saving the Books of Iraq.* New York: Knopf, 2004.

Winter, Jeanette. *The Librarian of Basra: A True Story from Iraq.* New York: Harcourt, 2004.

Web Sites

AASL (American Association of School Librarians) KCTools
http://www.ala.org/ICONN/kctools.html
For a site that explains the four phases of the research process

Library of Congress
http://www.loc.gov
For information from the largest library in the world

Multnomah County Library Homework Center
http://www.multcolib.org/homework
For an index of thousands of Web sites to use for homework

University of California-Berkeley Library, General Guides
http://www.lib.berkeley.edu/Help/guides.html
For online guides about finding information on the Internet and
evaluating Web sites

Places to Write

American Library Association
Public Information Office
50 East Huron Street
Chicago, IL 60611

Canadian Library Association
328 Frank Street
Ottawa, ON K2P 0X8
Canada

Library of Congress
101 Independence Avenue, SE
Washington, DC 20540

Index

About the Authors

Alice Flanagan has written more than one hundred titles for children and teachers, including holiday books, phonics for beginning readers, career guidance books, biographies of U.S. presidents and first ladies, and informational books about famous people and events in American history. Ms. Flanagan lives with her husband in Chicago, Illinois. As a writer/photographer team, they have published several books together. Their travels have taken them to interesting places and brought them many lifelong friends.

Emily J. Dolbear has been an editor at Franklin Watts, Children's Press, The Ecco Press, and Editorial Directions. She now works as a freelance editor and writer in Brookline, Massachusetts, where she lives with her husband and sons, Joseph and Marco.